What Most Business Owners Don't Know...

And Will Never Know...

About Internet Marketing

Discover many low or no-cost Internet lead generation tactics that you can begin using today to double your marketing results immediately.

By

John North

EVOLVE SYSTEMS GROUP PTY LTD

www.evolveyourbusiness.com.au

ideas@evolveyourbusiness.com.au

All rights reserved. No part of this book may be reproduced or transmitted in any form or by any means, electronic or mechanical, including photocopying, recording or by any information storage and retrieval system, without written permission from the authors, except for the inclusion of brief quotations in a review.

Limit of Liability Disclaimer: The information contained in this book is for information purposes only, and may not apply to your situation. The author, publisher, distributor and provider provide no warranty about the content or accuracy of content enclosed. Information provided is subjective. Keep this in mind when reviewing this guide.

Neither the Publisher nor Authors shall be liable for any loss of profit or any other commercial damages resulting from use of this guide. All links are for information purposes only and are not warranted for content, accuracy, or any other implied or explicit purpose.

Earnings Disclaimer: All income examples in this book are just that – examples. They are not intended to represent or guarantee that everyone will achieve the same results. You understand that each individual's success will be determined by his or her desire, dedication, background, effort and motivation to work. There is no guarantee you will duplicate any of the results stated here. You recognize any business endeavour has inherent risk of loss of capital.

"The typical result one can expect to achieve is nothing. The "typical" person never gets to the end of this book. The "typical" person fails to implement anything. Thus they earn nothing. Zero. No income. And perhaps a loss of income. That's because "typical" people do nothing and therefore they achieve nothing. Be atypical. Do something. Implement something. If it doesn't work; make a change…and implement that. Try again…try harder. Persist. And reap the rewards."

Copyright © 2014 by John North

ISBN:1500808393

Contents

About the Author ... XI

Our Passion to help business owners succeed in marketing ... XIII

Foreword ... XV

INTRODUCTION

What is Internet Marketing & How is it Different ... 1

    What is Internet Marketing? ... 2

    How it differs from Traditional Marketing ... 2

CHAPTER ONE

Why Should Your Company Engage in Internet Marketing? ... 4

    Convenience ... 5

    Ease of Management ... 5

    Cost Effectiveness ... 6

    Wider Reach ... 7

    Ease of Customization ... 7

    Stronger Relationships ... 8

    Swift Data Collection ... 9

    Higher ROI On Your Website ... 9

    The Ability To Discover New Markets ... 10

    Extensive Competitor Analysis ... 10

    Demographic Targeting ... 11

CHAPTER TWO

The Core Components of Internet Marketing ... 14

    1) Website Design and Development ... 14

    2) Blog ... 16

    Engaging Customers ... 16

    Link Building 16
3) SEO (Search Engine Optimization) 17
    Always Use Quality Content 17
    Research Industry Keywords 18
    Include Long Tailed Keywords 18
4) Email Marketing 18
    Send Out Friendly Messages 19
    Keep Your Messages Limited 19
5) Social Media Presence 20
6) Analytics 21
    It's All About The Numbers 22
    What Do Browsers Have to Do with This? 22
    Words are important 23
    Change is Important 23
    Website Development 24
    Blog 24
    SEO 24
    Email Marketing 25
    Social Media 25
    Analytics 25

CHAPTER THREE

What Are the Different Types of Internet Marketing? 26
  Search Engine Marketing 26
  Pay per Click Advertising (PPC Advertising) ... 27
  Referral Marketing 27
  Inbound Marketing 28
  Affiliate Marketing 29
  Video Marketing 29
  Podcast Marketing 30
  Conversion Marketing 30
  Viral Marketing 31

CHAPTER FOUR

How to Start Your Internet Marketing	34
For Your Website Design	34
Have a Plan	34
Design and Use a Professional Logo	35
Include Social Share Buttons	35
Work on Navigation	35
Call to Action	36
Mobile Optimization	36
Limit the Number of Pages	37
For Your Blog	37
Personalize Your 'About Me' Page	37
Create a Powerful Network	38
Grab Attention with Content	38
Don't Stuff Keywords	39
For SEO Building	39
Focus on Quality Not Quantity	39
Create Link-Worthy Content	40
Don't Forget to Link Your Inner Pages	41
Time Your Emails Carefully	42
Improve Your Signup Process	42
Limit Your Email Receivers	43
Allow Subscribers to Opt Out	43
Keep Up With Your Competitors	44
Test Your Email Marketing	44
For Your Social Media	45
Post Popular Content	45
Limit the Number of Your Social Media Profiles	46
Always Answer Queries	46
Include Images on Your Posts	47
Become an Expert	48
For Your Analytics	48
Set Your Goals	49
Manage Your Data	49
Set Up Video Event Tracking	49
Focus on Internal Searches	50

Check if All Your Pages are Being Tracked ... 50

CHAPTER FIVE

Things You Should Be Cautious About in Internet Marketing ... 52

1. Not Having a Strategy ... 52
2. Not Knowing Your Audience ... 53
3. Not Listening Before You Speak ... 53
4. Not Paying Attention to Web Analytics ... 53
5. Not Combining the Elements of Internet Marketing ... 54
6. Not Making Social Connections ... 54
7. Not Having Good Offers and Calls to Action ... 55
8. Not Considering Load Time ... 55
9. Not Using Viral Marketing ... 56
10. Not Trying Out New Opportunities ... 56

CHAPTER SIX

Myths and Facts Surrounding Internet Marketing ... 58

Myth #1: My Target Market Is Older So I Don't Need Social Media ... 58
Myth #2: Email Marketing Doesn't Work Anymore ... 58
Myth #3: Anyone Can Build My Website ... 59
Myth #4: Great Internet Marketing Gets Instant Results ... 59
Myth #5: Facebook Is All You Need ... 60
Myth #6: Internet Marketing Is Only For Big Companies ... 60
Myth #7: You Don't Need Money for Internet Marketing ... 61
Myth #8: You Need To Be On the First Page of Google ... 61

CHAPTER SEVEN

How to Keep Track of Your Internet Marketing ... 63

Tip #1: Ask Your Customers	63
Tip #2: Subscribe to Google Alerts	64
Tip #3: Consider Using Trackable Phone Numbers and Others	64
Tip #4: Use Blog Search	65
Tip #5: Try Out Social Mention	65
Tip #7: Track Landing Pages	65
Tip #8: Keep Tabs with Tools like Hootsuite and Sendible	66
Tip #9: Use Specialized Tools like SEO Monitor	66
Tips #10: Benefit From Sentiment Metrics	66

CHAPTER EIGHT

THE LATEST TRENDS OF INTERNET MARKETING	68
Content Matters to Google	68
Focus on Mobile Devices	69
Design is Crucial	69
Video, Video, Video	70
Rely on Social Media Audiences	70
Keep Up With Google	71
Try Out HTML 5	71
Show Your Interest with Pinterest	72
Less is More	72
Age of Ad Retargeting	73
Interconnectivity of Social Signals and SEO	73
Email Marketing Has Reemerged	74
Loyalty Marketing in Focus	75
Innovative Changes	75
Increased Use of Gamification	76

CHAPTER NINE

ENHANCING YOUR CURRENT INTERNET MARKETING	81
Post Daily Content on Social Media	81

Run a Campaign	82
Consider Running a Twitter Q&A	82
Experiment with Blog Titles	83
Let Infographics Take Charge	83
Improve Customer Services	84
Embrace Mistakes and Errors	85
Change the Formatting and Appearance of Your Content	85
Send Out an Email Newsletter	86
Hire a Public Relations Agency	87
Create Business Cards with your Website URL	87
Add an FAQ Section to Your Website	88
CONCLUSION	91
RESOURCES & REFERENCES	93

REGISTER THIS BOOK NOW and I'll immediately gift you my action packed, comprehensive and life changing four part video course… **absolutely FREE**…no strings attached!

In it, amongst a literal slew of other fact-packed ideas, you'll learn the inside secrets of how to generate as many leads as your business can handle… WITHOUT spending a cent on marketing or advertising. Interested?

Come on, action this right now. Don't take the chance of deferring and then forgetting!

Visit http://bookoffer.evolveyourbusiness.com.au or

Scan this QR Code:

Do it now and I'll see you in a couple of minutes when we will commence our exciting journey into the world of Internet Marketing!

ABOUT THE AUTHOR

John North is a versatile and well-rounded entrepreneur with a solid background in Accounting, Banking, Finance, Personal Development IT, Marketing and Business Management.

John currently holds a number of titles, including CEO of Evolve Systems Group, Associate Diploma in Business (Accounting) and Fellow of the Institute of Public Accountants.

John's passion is to help business owners become more strategic and smarter about their marketing efforts. He constantly pushes the envelope of what's possible in this modern era and is widely regarded amongst his peers as very innovative and highly creative in his approach.

John lives in Sydney, Australia and is an active squash player and student of all things marketing and technology.

Our Passion to help business owners succeed in marketing

In the digital era of the business world, internet marketing is the ruling king. Not only does it broaden a company's reach and ensure its brand's visibility, but it can also generate prospects and even turn them into loyal consumers. Evolve Your Business understood this before the rest, marking it as one of the pioneering internet marketing companies in Australia.

Led by John North, Evolve Your Business is a network of services that aims at offering a one-stop internet marketing solution to businesses in Australia and New Zealand. Its current network includes:

- Internet Marketing and Business Strategy (www.evolveyourbusiness.com.au)
- Evolve Mobile Apps (www.evolvemobile.com.au)
- Evolve Hosting and Web Design

   (www.evolvehosting.com.au)
- Evolve CRM (Cloud and On Site)

   (www.evolvecrm.com.au)
- Evolve Payroll (www.evolvepay.com.au)

John and his company have always aimed at customer satisfaction, which is why the prices offered are affordable while services and packages are comprehensive.

John can be reached at his personal website at www.johnnorth.com.au or email ideas@evolveyourbusiness.com.au

FOREWORD

This is the first book on Internet marketing that has actually shown me how all the pieces of the Internet marketing puzzle are put together.

I have read a ton of books that tell you how you should position your business with LinkedIn and how to use Facebook for advertising. Books about Search Engine Optimization, Pinterest and social media marketing, to name just a few. These books tell you what you should be doing but unfortunately they don't show you how to do it. John's book –*What Most Business Owners Don't Know…And Will Never Know…About Internet Marketing* is just that. It is the book that will guide you through the internet marketing maze and it will show you how to change the way you do business.

After reading this book I have a far better understanding of how it all fits together and also how to successfully market my business via the internet and social media. I have also gained enough knowledge from the book to know that you must engage the services of a professional in this area. I have heard so many disaster stories about the failure of internet marketing and that's why you must ensure you hire the right professional. And that's the other great thing about this book. It provides the business owner with a checklist to use when selecting the internet professional who will bring the best results for their business.

Peter Lawson
CEO Biz Connections Australia
Number # 1 Best Selling Author of the highly acclaimed book:
New Business Breakthrough Strategies - 9 Proven Business Strategies to Boost Profit Margin

INTRODUCTION

What is Internet Marketing & How is it Different from Traditional Marketing?

Marketing has been around for a long time now. In fact, traders have been using marketing to attract customers for thousands of years. However, like everything else, marketing has come a long way since then and evolved to such an extent that the entire dynamics of marketing have changed.

Today, the marketing methods used are more efficient than ever. It really is quite simple for a business to get its message across to its target audience…and fast!

The purpose of marketing remains the same, i.e. convince people to perform a desired action, which is usually buying a product. However, the methods of accomplishing these goals have evolved and a lot of subtlety has entered the fray.

Although print marketing ruled the roost for decades in the past, visual marketing took off with the advent of television. Now even television is going the way of the dinosaur since digital marketing began to spawn. People spend more time online than they do watching TV or reading the newspaper. To combat the diminishing TV market manufacturers are making all their models internet ready. Is it any wonder that the internet is the new battleground for marketers?

"For any business to succeed in the current era using internet marketing isn't an option any longer, it's an absolute must!" Before you learn how to use internet marketing in the following chapters, you need a thorough introduction to internet marketing and a comparison between it and traditional marketing methods and techniques.

What is Internet Marketing?

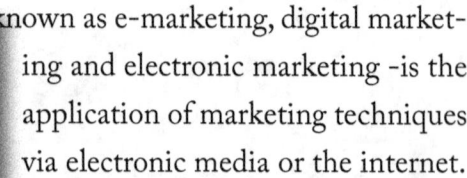

known as e-marketing, digital marketing and electronic marketing -is the application of marketing techniques via electronic media or the internet.

Companies that are marketing their brand over the internet are involved in online marketing. However, you should understand that the marketing responses used in online marketing are both direct and indirect. This is because potential customers often don't know they are being targeted with ads and other marketing content. As mentioned before, marketing is much more subtle now.

How it differs from Traditional Marketing

The primary difference between traditional marketing and internet marketing is that the latter has the ability to reach a large number of people…and blindingly fast… because it isn't limited by geography. On the other hand, traditional marketing, no matter how widely used or circulated, is never able to reach to a vast number of people at once and usually nowhere near as quick.

However, no difference is as notable as traditional marketing's in ability to provide direct and exact feedback about the outcomes of its efforts. However internet marketing provides companies with data that is collected once the initial ad impression has been made. Though these statistics aren't always true to the last number (because the situation is ever changing), they are extremely accurate and can be relied upon.

Because we live in a tougher world economy where global competition is fierce, it is crucial for businesses around the world to keep an eye on their return on investment (ROI) through various marketing channels; that's why business managers and owners require fast and accurate numbers which show them the result of their marketing efforts.

True, traditional marketing isn't obsolete, but the emphasis has very definitely changed to digital marketing and this will only increase. If you doubt that just ask the newspaper barons whose "rivers of gold" via newspaper advertising have all but dried up. If you are running a business, regardless of size, you have to use internet marketing to establish your brand in the market and both attract, inform and service more customers.

The purpose of this Book is to educate and encourage business owners and managers on the main aspects of internet marketing so that you can learn, and apply, the key principles along with your traditional marketing techniques to literally leapfrog your competitors whilst generating substantially more sales, profits and cash.

Interested?

Thought so, let's begin.

CHAPTER ONE

Why Should Your Company Engage in Internet Marketing?

Internet marketing has now become a necessity as part of your marketing strategies. Without Internet Marketing it's highly unlikely your company can increase sales or revenues. **Fact:** more than 50% of buyers wanting recently released and/or high value products first turn to social media to conduct their preliminary research.

On the basis of "fish where the fish are biting", doesn't it make sense to have an online presence where people can give you a "lookover"?

Yes, implementing internet marketing in your business enables you to build relationships with your customers and manage them for literally cents in the dollar.

Truly, there are hundreds of reasons why you simply must pay much more attention to internet marketing and Ill discuss a few of them now and do remember, at the core of each suggestion, we are really discussing ways to ramp up sales profits and cash…and do so quickly and effortlessly, once you know how.

Convenience

Your internet marketing efforts not only make things a lot more convenient for your customers, but also for your business. As your customers can browse your online retail store 24/7 and from any part of the world, your bricks and mortar business doesn't even need to be open. Sales can happen as you are in dreamland, or the local coffee shop, wherever.

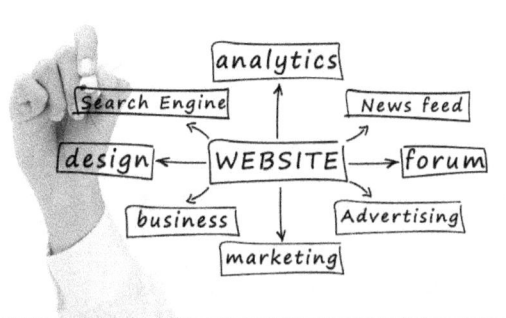

It's convenient for them and for you. Whenever they want and from whichever device they choose, you won't have to worry about regular retail store hassles like opening or closing your business at specified times. Your store will be accessible to your customers throughout and you will earn even when you're tucked up in your bed. Even though implementing internet marketing strategies may require some effort from you in the beginning, it will be able to draw in great profits once you develop a proper and functional strategy.

EASE OF MANAGEMENT

Good quality internet programs allow you to manage with ease and unlike traditional marketing, changin the strategy or plan can be made quickly even when you're away from your office vacationing with your family or simply taking a day off.

Anyone who has used traditional marketing such as advertisements and billboards knows it takes a lot of time to make even the smallest changes to their strategy, making the whole process tiring and draining to boot. With internet marketing, once you decided on the strategy change, it's almost as instantaneous as a flick of the button. And even if you feel you don't have the expertise in the field of internet marketing, you can always hire a professional agency or company to guide you in the right direction.

Cost Effectiveness

Even if you have developed a great business website, it can only take you to a certain level if you don't make the effort to implement the right marketing techniques to increase its visibility. Internet marketing is an extremely cost effective option for promoting your business. It has the power to boost the promotion dynamics of your business without burdening your pockets.

Acts like sending promotional newsletters, optimizing your website for search engines, and availing pay per click (PPC) programs can be amazingly affordable and cost effective. Some of these benefits are even available for free. With this in mind, you will realize that internet marketing is a lot better than the former.

WIDER REACH

Another reason why many big and small organizations have taken up internet marketing is because they are aware that it 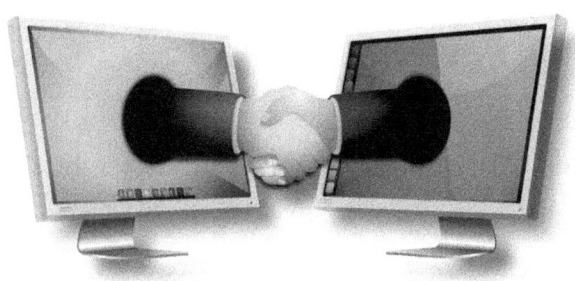 can reach a large number of people at any given time. Because online advertisements and marketing have a global reach, even customers at the very far end of the world can communicate with you without any trouble. With the help of the internet and a properly implemented internet marketing strategy, you can easily eradicate the geographical limitations and access a pool of clients. Moreover, with these online programs, you can increase the prospects of your business and begin growing and prospering.

EASE OF CUSTOMIZATION

Digital or online marketing is all about personalization. Thanks to different techniques, your business can personalize its offers, promotions, and products to a customer according to their preference and purchase history. Businesses that have engaged in internet marketing know that  they can make targeted services according to their clienteles' preferences simply by tracking the web pages they visit. The information you collect from these tracking websites can even help you plan cross selling campaigns so you can increase your chances of sale. A lot of websites such as Amazon also use their targeting programs to recommend similar products to those customers have added to their cart. These smart tactics are also used by software download websites, which is why they show you other products that were purchased or downloaded by others like you.

Stronger Relationships

Yet another reason for you to adopt internet marketing strategies as soon as you can is their power to build new relationships with potential clients and increase the value of your brand in the eyes of your existing customers. Once a customer purchases a product from you, you can begin building an everlasting relationship by sending them

an email to confirm their order and thank them for their purchase. Many multi-national companies also email their customers regularly about special offers, promotions and new products as it helps them stay on their customers' minds and maintain the relationship they created with them.

Aside from using emails, many organizations invite and ask their loyal customers to write product reviews or guest posts for their website. All of these efforts combined will allow you to strengthen the bonds with your online customers and ensure that they come back to you regularly.

Swift Data Collection

A major setback traditional marketing and advertising users face is the inability to collect the data that helps them know the results of their efforts. Every time your customer interacts and transacts with your company online or clicks on an online ad, the action will be captured and noted.

As a business, you can use this information in a number of ways. For example, many businesses use this information to know the percentage of products and services that have been sold, whereas others use the data to divide their customers according to purchases. Both of these techniques help businesses send out promotional materials and ultimately increase their business. Even though there is a lot of controversy involving the amount of data that is being collected from various customers, this information can prove to be invaluable if used in the correct way.

Higher ROI On Your Website

There are many websites and online businesses that don't have a clue why they are not receiving returns on investment (ROI) even after creating a fairly good website or retail store. The answer to this question is simple. These businesses have focused only

on their website and not on internet marketing and its many aspects. However, the businesses which have worked on creating a simple and professional websites and promoted their brand and products online have been able to ensure a good ROI on their website. Because internet marketing is ever changing and developing by leaps and bounds, it is important that you use the newest strategies and keep up with trends. An easy way to promote your website throughout the internet is by submitting articles in various directories and via social networking websites, a technique that is known as SEO or Search Engine Optimization (more about this will be discussed in chapter #2).

The Ability To Discover New Markets

The main objective or goal of any marketing strategy is to discover new markets and prospects for the business. With internet marketing, you can hope to do exactly that. The advertisements you place on the internet will draw a lot of traffic to your website, which will then help you in converting your website visitors into clients. If you engage in SEO aggressively, you can easily secure millions of viewers and reach a large chunk of your target audience within a couple of months. With a considerable number of customers throughout the world, you can expand your business and reach out to an even bigger market.

Extensive Competitor Analysis

If you are involved in internet marketing, you will also make an effort to analyse your competitors and their respective online strategies. As a growing business, you can be informed about the products being released or price changes or identify the secondary market that your competitor is communicating with. Therefore, adopting internet marketing will help you stay abreast with your  competitors' strategies and ensure that you provide at least identical services if not improved ones.

Demographic Targeting

Internet marketing also gives you the chance to target different demographic regions and measure their collective responses. Basically, this kind of targeting allows you to target those who are more likely to buy your product or services. One way to collect demographic data is to ask your customers and prospects to fill out a questionnaire on your website so that you can identify their ages, genders and interests. All of this information combined will help you provide services that suit your cus-

Now that you have learned about the top benefits of internet marketing, it's time to educate yourself about some of the most basic and crucial components of this type of marketing. This is important because unless you know what these components are and how they can be implemented, you won't be able to have an effective internet marketing strategy. So, without further ado, move on to the next chapter and discover the components of internet marketing.

Facebook advertising is a very precise example of how you can target specific demographics. When you place a Facebook advertisement you can choose what age, sex, location, likes, marital status you want to target. For example you could target engaged women below 27 in a specific suburb.

Chapter Summary

Internet marketing has its own unique benefits and perks. Here is a brief look at the features that make this marketing method one of the top around.

1. **Convenient**: *Internet marketing is convenient for your customers as well as your business. For your customers, it gives them the convenience of finding out about your products without any time or place restrictions.*

2. **Easier to Manage**: *One of the biggest benefits of internet marketing is that once it is set up, it is very easy and simple to manage.*

3. **Lighter on Your Pocket:** *So many businesses have started to turn towards internet marketing because it is extremely cost effective and doesn't need a very large and overwhelming budget.*

4. **Bigger Reach:** *Internet marketing reaches a larger number of people because there are no geographical barriers to it. It doesn't matter where your business is located because your customer could be sitting at the other end of the world and the internet it would help them know about your products in an instant.*

5. **Customizable:** *Because of the different techniques used in internet marketing, you can personalize your promotions and the offers that you provide according to your business and its requirements.*

6. **Easy Data Collection**: *Unlike conventional marketing, this type of marketing will give you an actual analysis of the results of your efforts.*

7. **Chance to Discover New Markets:** *The billboards and advertisements that you place on roads and bridges are still not able to reach a worldwide audience. This is why a lot of businesses can't seem to discover new markets.*

CHAPTER TWO

The Core Components of Internet Marketing

Because of the importance and demand for internet marketing, there are more than a hundred aspects and elements that any business has to consider when implementing it. However, even though the field is quite vast, there are only six core components that you need to remember. Without any of these components, you cannot even start to devise a marketing strategy let alone carry it through. In this section, we talk about these six components in detail.

1) Website Design and Development

Your website is the face of your company, which means it needs to be professional, user friendly, and tidy. Therefore, because website designs and development give any website a higher chance of success, you must make sure you are making a good and professional first impression.

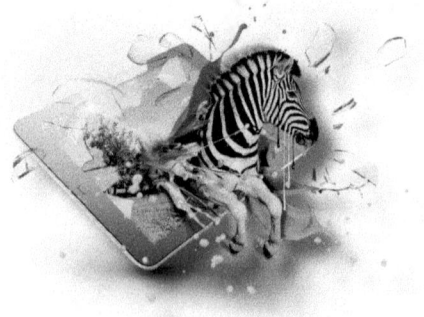

When designing a new website or redesigning an old one, one thing you can do is hire an affordable yet expert professional or company to get you started. Once you have it set up, it will be a lot easier for you to manage and control your website.

Whether you are developing a website of your own or asking a professional service to do it, an essential factor that you cannot forget is planning. You will also require good communication and a well-designed and thorough internet marketing strategy after the site has been completed. However, the latter two come later.

When planning, the first few things you need to do are to determine your target audience, define the goal of your website, come up with your branding or logo message, and decide how you plan on implementing all of these on your professional website.

Finally, when designing a website meant to attract customers, you should focus greatly on its functionality. Even though the design is what will originally attract visitors, functionality is what will keep them there. Therefore, if everything looks pretty but isn't functioning properly, your visitors won't stay. They may even prefer going to your competitors for the services they need. So don't make the mistake of ignoring your website design and features when developing a proper internet marketing strategy.

Some ideas for a checklist for a new website prior to launch:

1. Check entire website for spelling errors.
2. Check that the website displays properly in all known browsers.
3. Has a favicon been created? If so ensure it displays correctly. A favicon is the small icon that appears in your browser tab.
4. Test the website on different monitor resolutions.
5. Is the website mobile friendly?
6. Do any web forms go to the correct email address?
7. Do all external links work especially social media?

2) Blog

One of the most influential tools you need for your internet marketing strategy is a blog. When blogging was first developed, it was used to speak one's mind and share ideas with others. Today, however, the scenario has changed quite dramatically and blogging is used by several online businesses for different reasons. Blogs have the power to increase a business' income and boost its growth. To give you a better idea of why businesses choose blogs, here are two of their top advantages.

Engaging Customers

If you want people to buy your products or services, you need to build their trust as well as the authority of your brand in your industry. If you fail to do this, people won't buy from you no matter how great your offers and services. One way to increase your authority is to blog. With your words, people will realize that you know what you're doing. Moreover, when you blog, your readers may respond to your articles with praise, critiques, and questions. All of these will help you know more about what they need and eventually deliver it.

Link Building

Your company blog is a fantastic source for links. With the right kind of content, you can place links that go back to your own website. Just remember using keyword-rich links and target-specific key phrases make it easier for your customers to find you. Moreover, with the right kind of posts, you will be able to attract your customers' attention and, if they really like your blog and what you have to say, get them to link your posts on their social media pages, which will give you even more credibility in the industry.

Blogging is an essential tool for the success of your business and implementing it as part of your internet marketing strategy is the only way you can achieve the goals you have set for yourself.

3) SEO (Search Engine Optimization)

If you want your blog, website, and social media accounts to appear on the first pages of Google or other search engines, be sure to use SEO in a balanced but effective way. Many of your potential customers will start looking for the things they need through search engines. So having search engine optimized pages will help you become noticed and your website will get a higher rank that which makes you more visible to people seeking your type of products or services. Even though the SEO area is quite large and covers a lot of ground, there are some basic tips and methods you can start with.

Always Use Quality Content

Even if you include targeted keywords and phrases in your content, your site won't receive the attention it needs until its content is of high quality. Therefore, whether you are writing the blog or website content on your own or have hired someone to do it, always make sure to check and recheck the content for spelling mistakes, conceptual errors, and other issues that can turn off your readers and reduce your rankings. Visit www.evolveacademy.com.au for a free video course on creating great marketing messages for your websites and marketing materials.

Research Industry Keywords

Before you begin to implement SEO in your marketing strategy, you must first be sure you have done ample research on the keywords that needs to be used in your content. An easy way to find these keywords is to find out the most used keywords or phrases for your industry and then use or buy them. You can take a look at the blogs and websites of your competitors and see how they build their SEO for inspiration.

Include Long Tailed Keywords

Aside from industry keywords, you also need to use long tailed keywords or phrases in your content. Even though such keywords should only be used sparingly, they are essential because they help in specifying your business in the industry. Most businesses develop long tailed keywords by adding the location or city where they operate to the original keyword they use.

As this is the age of the internet, you will be making a big mistake if you don't implement SEO in your internet marketing. Even if you are just starting out and haven't realized the importance of this technology yet, it is about time you know that your business cannot survive without it.

4) Email Marketing

One of the most preferred internet marketing tools used by a variety of businesses is email marketing. If you are able to correctly and successfully carry out an email marketing campaign, this technique will help you in generating more leads for your online business. This method is the most beneficial in e-marketing because it keeps you on the minds of your customers even when they can't visit your website or blog.

Here are a few tricks you can use when working on the email marketing component.

Send Out Friendly Messages

The first tip you need to use is to send out friendly messages that are interesting for your customers to read. Be sure to put most of your effort into your welcome message; if it is cold and rigid, it will reflect badly on your email campaign and you will lose your audience. That aside, every email you send should be personalized so that readers can feel connected to what you are saying.

Keep Your Messages Limited

If you don't want your emails to end up in the spam folder, you must control the amount of emails that you send. Even though the email campaign will help you in generating more business, too many emails will lead to you losing your credibility. Ideally, your emails should be sent out one to two times in a week (depending on your target audience) so that your customers actually look forward to them instead of feeling hassled.

When implemented correctly, your email marketing techniques won't only help you in growing your business, but they will also increase your credibility and value in the eyes of your customer.

5) Social Media Presence

It's important for you to own your social media space. Each platform tends to name the login or address after your business. For example ABC Flyers would have an address of www.facebook.com/abcflyers. However someone else could claim if first causing you to have to name it slightly differently. Even if your business is not active on a particular platform, it doesn't hurt to register and claim your spot. Google+ actually takes time to offer its page name so be sure to check back to claim it.

The major population of the world is using social media websites and platforms such as Facebook, Twitter, Linked In, Vimeo, YouTube, Google+, and Pinterest. Even small businesses have begun to realize that they have no chance of getting ahead and beating their competitors without a professionally maintained Facebook and Twitter group or page. Now the best thing about most of these social media platforms is that they are free and don't really need a lot of effort or time to be set up. And once these business accounts have been created, all you need to do is manage them properly to reap benefits like the ones listed below.

The first thing social media helps you with is stay in the thoughts of your customers constantly by posting status updates, blog posts, informational posts, etc. Because people spend several hours on social media on any given day, you have a higher probability of reaching out to them and making yourself heard.

One of the primary reasons small businesses go for social media is because it helps them create a community of their existing and potential customers. The discussions and interactions that will take place on the page or profile will be about your company. So expect to receive a lot of feedback from your customers about the services or products you provide.

Finally, among all the other components of internet marketing, this is the only one to help you reach out to exponential numbers of people. Facebook and Twitter feeds and information are viral in nature; so if you post something interesting or really useful on your social account, your customers are likely to share and talk about it with other friends and family members.

Internet marketing through social media is an excellent way to make your business' brand visible and ultimately increase the number of customers who use the services you provide. So if you haven't yet begun using social media for your business get started and make the most of it before your competitors control the industry.

6) Analytics

Analytics has its own set of pros and cons. Although the metrics and measurements obtained in analytics can be invaluable and ideal for fine-tuning your website, they can also be very overwhelming and confusing. So the question is why should you bother implementing analytics in your internet marketing strategy? The answer to this question lies in the following points.

It's All About The Numbers

Analytics is all about measurements and numbers. There are a number of services such as Google Webmaster tools or Google Analytics that can help you work around these and answer important questions linked to your internet marketing plan, such as:

How many people visited my website?

How often did an individual visit the website?

How long did the individual stay?

What browser is the individual using?

What is the one web page that is visited the most on the website?

With these numbers, you will have deeper insight as to what your target market likes, would rather you didn't have on your website, and other criteria that can help ensure your success in the virtual world.

What Do Browsers Have to Do with This?

After checking the previous list, one question business people may have on their minds is, "Why do we need to keep track of what browsers people use to view the website?" The answer to this is straightforward. You need to know which browser the visitor is using because the pages that are displayed across them are not the same.

Though the differences may only be slight with little changes in some pixels here and there, they will make the site's user experience completely different. On the other hand, the differences are very large at times, making the entire website look unprofessional and even throwing the entire alignment of the page into disarray.

If you use analytics, it will pinpoint the browsers where bounce rates are highest and help you make your website friendlier towards your target market.

Words are important

It's vital that once you begin driving traffic to your website you monitor your keywords. Without a base point of where you started its difficult later to gauge your marketing effectiveness. There are many SEO online applications that can do this.

Change is Important

Analytics can be tricky to set up and interpret and a lot trickier to manage if you don't have the right set of skills. Change and at least a few alterations are unavoidable no matter how perfect the initial analytics strategy is. After all, trends are ever changing.

Investing in analytics will help you get great benefits that will turn your business from a barely recognizable company to one of the top names in the industry.

Even though there are many combined elements responsible for a successful internet marketing strategy, the six basic ones mentioned here are the most crucial. Some tips and steps that will help you in improving each of these components are mentioned in chapter #4.

Before you learn how to properly implement these, however, it is important to discover the different kinds of internet marketing so that you can decide on the best strategy according to your business and its requirements.

Keeping track of your website rankings and search engine performance is vital. Check out www.evolveseo.com.au for a range of packages that can help you improve and manage your marketing activities.

Chapter Summary

As you have learned, internet marketing is made of many small but detailed features that are divided into six elements.

Website Development

Your business or company website is the one place your potential market and audience will visit when they need to discover your products. This is why your website must not only be professional, but also have quality content that is informative and useful for the client.

Blog

By now, you know what blogs are and exactly how important they are for internet marketing and reliability purposes. This is an influential tool that has the power to increase your net income and boost your company's growth.

SEO

Search engine optimization is necessary if you want your website or blog to appear on the first few pages of Google and other search engines. Through the chapter, you have discovered what SEO is and how you can use it for your benefit.

Email Marketing

You also learned that generating leads for your business with email marketing is simple and straightforward. If you are able to create friendly and concise email messages to your consisting customers, you will have a higher chance of getting noticed and increasing your online sales.

Social Media

No matter how small your business, you now realize the importance of having social media pages. Social media websites are one of the first places that your customers expect to find you. Divide your time intelligently between each of the websites that you are choosing and you'll be successful in attracting customers.

Analytics

Bringing in customers through your internet marketing is not the only thing you should do. You need to gather analytics that will tell you about the exact results that your internet marketing is able to achieve. If you didn't know why and how to use analytics before reading this Book, you do so now.

CHAPTER THREE

What Are the Different Types of Internet Marketing?

Before implementing internet or online marketing strategies to promote your business, it is crucial to know about the different types of internet marketing. There are close to a hundred marketing types to choose from, the one you select depends entirely on the nature of your products or services, budget, and the time you can afford to spend on it. Another thing you should know is that although some types work well independently, others are best used in with conjunction with other methods.

To get you set on the right path for online marketing, here are some of the basic online marketing types.

SEARCH ENGINE MARKETING

Search engine marketing (SEM) is a type of internet marketing which focuses on promoting the visibility of websites in search engine result pages. To pull this off, SEM uses a variety of techniques which include search engine optimization, strategic

content marketing, paid advertising, and social media networking. You will note here that SEO is also one of the six crucial components of internet marketing, so its value cannot be underestimated. With the correct SEO techniques and efforts, you will not only be able to promote your website, but your business as well. More about how you can do this is discussed later in the book.

Pay per Click Advertising (PPC Advertising)

A very popular type of internet marketing is pay per click advertising (PPC). In pay per click advertising, a web publisher such as a search engine presents advertising which only charges the advertiser for the number of times a visitor clicks on the ad to go to  the targeted website. In short, the advertiser is not paid for the number of times the advertisement is viewed.

Often you can locate special discount coupons for pay per click for Google and Bing which saves some money on your initial campaign. Creating campaigns can be complex and often it's a good idea to get someone who is an expert in this area to help. Alternatively there are a lot of courses and online information to be found.

Referral Marketing

Referral marketing is a simple and very subtle type of internet marketing. Referral marketing goes through a process which is explained below.

A website (your business) posts something like a blog or another interesting piece of information on a website or social media

One of the members of your target audience finds these posts particularly interesting and decides to 'refer' or share it with other people such as their friends and family members.

A chain reaction is created where your content goes from one individual to a much larger group of people.

Today, referral marketing is one of the most promising types of internet marketing mainly because people like sharing things on social media websites and other social platforms.

Also take a look at a new digital referral platform at www.evolveyourbusiness.com.au/referron/

Inbound Marketing

Inbound marketing is a method that draws attention and ultimately visits to a particular website by placing information on another website which others are looking for. This is done in several ways; for example, you may decide to provide valuable information through a blog or article posted on another website. The main purpose of inbound marketing is not to tell the reader about their products or services directly, but to provide them with specific content that the reader finds useful.

How is this beneficial for your business? Well, when a search engine user searches for a specific type of content, the website containing your content will be displayed. Even though it isn't directly related to your business or website, it will increase traffic on your website through secondary information. Websites where you will commonly find such marketing content include Ezine Articles and Squiddo.

A popular platform called Hubspot is very focused around Inbound Marketing.

Affiliate Marketing

Affiliate marketing refers to the type where a third party recommends a customer to a vendor or website. Businesses that engage in affiliate marketing market their own products and services through a website, but also have links on other websites that are not related to them but have similar interests for the consumers. Much like pay per click advertising, the affiliates are rewarded for the number of times a visitor from the primary website visits the secondary or 'affiliated' website.

Even though the results of affiliate marketing are not immediately recognizable, it does play a very significant role in e-retailers' marketing strategies.

Video Marketing

If you are not engaging or entertaining your customers in the new consumer world your business is at serious risk. Videos are especially handy for this strategy. When you market your products, services or brand using videos posted on YouTube, Vimeo or other such websites are great ways to drive traffic to your websites. Depending on the limitation of the website hosting the video, the videos that you post can vary in length, message, and content.

Several smart businesses have started using video marketing to tell their users about how to operate a particular product, which is particularly appreciated by viewers. Some of these businesses also inform their customers about parties or other such events that they will be hosting.

Podcast Marketing

Apple recently reported a milestone of over 1 billion podcast subscribers, this type of marketing can be a different way to reach potential customers. Podcasts have a 100% deliverability rate, once they have subscribed future episodes will be automatically delivered to their mobile device. Publishing on the Apple platform is free and a very easy process. Evolve Your Business also has a service that can help you publish and update your podcasts. Visit www.evolveyourbusiness.com.au for more information.

Also search Apple Podcasts for Evolve Your Business and Evolve Quickstart for examples of our work.

Conversion Marketing

This type of marketing involves direct interaction with your customers or audience. The main purpose of conversion marketing is to get feedback about a particular website, banner ad or landing from the audience and make changes accordingly. This kind of approach is often used for a marketing or PR campaign that aims at selling something new.

Conversion marketing can prove to be extremely beneficial for your business. One example of a conversion event other than a sale is if a customer were to abandon an online shopping cart, the company could market a special offer, e.g. free shipping, to convert the visitor into a paying customer.

Viral Marketing

This is a marketing method that uses social media networks to produce an increase in brand awareness or achieve other marketing objectives through either word-of-mouth or enhanced networking efforts on social media website. These viral promotions can also take the form of video clips, eBooks, images, interactive Flash games, apps, and much more. Understanding these methods and types will help you in better formulating an overall internet marketing strategy or your particular business or campaign.

Now that you have learned about the main types of internet marketing, here's a very important tip you should learn. When creating your strategy, don't just count on the channels mentioned here;

research the techniques being used by your competitors. Also learn the methods and techniques that would suit your business in the best way possible so that you have a comprehensive and well planned business and marketing strategy.

Chapter Summary

After explaining the basics of internet marketing, we explored its different types.

- **Search Engine Marketing:** *The main focus of SEM is to promote the visibility of your website in search engine result pages. This type of marketing pays special attention to SEO and optimizes blogs, social media profiles, and websites so their page ranks can increase.*

- **Pay per click advertising:** *If you engage in PPC or pay per click advertising, you will need to pay a web publisher for the number of times a visitor clicks on the ad that you have placed on their website. The benefit of this advertising is that you don't need to pay the advertiser when the ad has only been viewed.*

- **Referral Marketing:** *Referral marketing is where a particular website visitor or customer reads a post on one of your social media profiles or blog and shares it with their friends, followers, etc. In turn, these friend also like what you have to say and a chain reaction is created.*

- **Inbound Marketing:** *When your business posts non-promotional but informative articles, blogs or general content on other websites such as Ezine or Squiddo, you are engaging in inbound marketing. This type of marketing doesn't involve bragging* about your products, but rather telling the reader what they need to know.

- **Affiliate Marketing**: *As the name indicates, affiliate marketing is when your website is recommended by a third party to their customer or visitor. Businesses that are involved in affiliate marketing don't just sell their own products and services, but suggest the users of other related items as well.*

- **Video Marketing**: *Posting how-to and other such informational video content on YouTube is popularly known as video marketing. If your website has quality content combined with a well thought-out video marketing strategy, you'll be able to make a name for your brand quickly.*

- **Viral Marketing**: *The viral marketing method uses social media pages to bring about an increase in brand awareness and to achieve other marketing goals.*

- **Conversion Marketing**: *Conversion marketing makes you interact with your customers directly. In this type of marketing, you get feedback directly from your users about a certain website, ad or landing page.*

CHAPTER FOUR

How to Start Your Internet Marketing

After a quick overview of the top methods used for internet marketing, it is time to go back and elaborate on the six basic components (Website Design and Development, Blog, SEO, Email Marketing, Social Media, and Analytics) as they are the keys to establishing a marketing strategy. So, without further delay, here are the steps you need to start taking.

For Your Website Design

You probably have your own website already since that is one of the necessities of your business. However, you now need to tweak it a little. After all, the way that your website is laid out, the colors, fonts and images that it uses can mean the difference between the success and failure of your business. This is why you must make sure to avoid some of the most common mistakes made by web designers and developers today and make a professional website that your customers are happy to visit. Here are some tips which will help you in getting started.

Have a Plan

Before you even start designing or developing your website, you need to make sure that it meets the needs of your visitors effectively. This is why you need to map out your customer's journey from the moment they first visit your website to the time when they become a customer. Factors such as the design of the pages that they are going to view, the content they are going to read and the offers or promotions that are going to turn them into actual customers need to be decided beforehand.

Design and Use a Professional Logo

One of the most important things for your business as well as your website is using professional logo that represents your brand. Because your logo is such a crucial part of your company, you must make sure that you place it prominently on your website. You can also link your logo back to your home page so that visitors can easily navigate to it.

Include Social Share Buttons

The easier you make it for your audience to follow and share your content, the better your chances of making it big with your internet marketing strategy. However, don't make the mistake of implementing these share and follow buttons only on a couple of pages of your website. Instead, include them on every single page. These share buttons will also help your current customers tell their friends about your business, which will bring in the traffic that you require for your website.

Work on Navigation

Easy and hassle free navigation is essential in creating a good user experience. So when designing your website, identify the one factor that attracts and engages customers and work on it. The worst thing that you can do to your visitors is to greet them with a website where they cannot find anything. For this reason, it is important that you develop a platform that is simple and straightforward.

Call to Action

Make sure you have a call to action for your visitors. Often websites have substantial information but lack the basic concept of what to do next. Display your telephone number at the top right of the page. Don't make it hard for your potential customers to contact you! If you email us ideas@evolveyourbusiness.com.au we can send you a link to our special "Website Lead Conversion Evaluator".

Mobile Optimization

If you haven't yet optimized your website for a mobile device, you are surely missing out on a lot. According to recent studies, more than 80.5% of website visitors are now accessing their favorite website through a mobile device. So if you really want to tailor your site to fit the needs and requirements of your visitors, make sure that you make it possible for them to access your website through devices other than the personal computer.

Limit the Number of Pages

If your primary goal is to simplify your website and make it easier for visitors to navigate, the first thing that you need to do is to reduce the number of pages that people explore and click. If you can, get rid of unnecessary pages or fuse similar pages into one. This practice won't only help your visitors with navigation, it will also cut down your site's load time, which is a major factor in ensuring good user experience. Also make sure that you reduce the number of drop down menus as these have been reported as a nuisance for many visitors and websites.

FOR YOUR BLOG

Even though social media platforms such as Facebook and Twitter enjoy immense popularity, blogs are still a very crucial part of business and internet marketing. In fact, these internet marketing tools are no longer just an option for businesses as consumers and search engines alike view them to assess a company's worth and expertise. So, after integrating a blog into your site or dusting off your existing one, here are a few things that will help you make it the talk of the internet.

Personalize Your 'About Me' Page

If you look at some blog statistics, you'll discover that the About Me page is the most visited page after the main one. Because your readers want to know who are and what you do before reading what you have to say, you should invest your time in making a personal impression that will get you in their good books.

When writing the content for the About Me page, make sure that you don't sound robotic as this will leave a negative impact on the reader. Instead, be natural and try to appeal to the human side of your readers.

Generally it's a good idea to write this page in the style of what you can do for your visitors and less about your company history.

Create a Powerful Network

The two things that will make your blog noticeable include great content and a powerful network of likeminded people. To form a powerful blog network and following, you shouldn't limit yourself to writing things linked to your products. Expand within your niche and always look for fun and interesting facts as people escape the real world to the virtual one for the purpose of shedding away all seriousness. Once you have a good and strongly knitted network, you can ask your readers to join in and contribute to the blog as well.

Grab Attention with Content

Your website or business blog is all about the content. If you have something interesting and intriguing to say to your reader, they will have the time to listen to you. Some of the best ways to grab your readers are using catchy titles and  headlines, creating great opening paragraphs, and ending the blog with a powerful note.

So even though it is important that you focus on other factors of your blog, improving your content must always be your first objective.

Don't Stuff Keywords

Yes, keyword implementation is essential when you want your blog address to appear in the top search results of Google, but too much of a good thing can go against you. So even though experts suggest that you add relevant keywords to all your blog posts, you should avoid integrating more than 3-5 keywords per blog.

Also make sure that you only use keywords that are appropriate to your industry and business. This may mean spending time, effort and energy on searching and analyzing keywords, but you will be rewarded when your blog gets a high page rank.

For SEO Building

Link building and search engine optimization have been around for more than a decade now. Even though Google may seem to be the only search engine you should focus your efforts on, other search engines such as Yahoo and Bing have embraced this trend and expect to see it in their search results. So, in order for you to get maximum exposure online, you need to implement the following to maximize the results of your efforts and results.

Focus on Quality Not Quantity

Every now and then, Google changes its algorithm and millions of websites lose their rankings overnight. How do you stop this from happening to your website? Well, though there are a number of things you can try out; one of the best techniques is to focus on the quality of your content instead of the quantity.

If you have a blog page and decide to post even one top notch quality post, then it will prove to be a lot better than 100 low quality ones. You must also avoid using ancient link building techniques such as mass directory submissions because Google's algorithm no longer

supports or takes note of these. In fact, if you are not careful, your page may end up being labeled 'spammy' because Google will automatically think that you are a fraud.

Create Link-Worthy Content

When creating the content for SEO purposes, you must make sure that it is link-worthy. If you post poor quality content on your blog or website, bounce rates will increase, causing your Google rankings to drop down. To sum it all up, if you provide quality and valuable content to your readers, they will be more likely to hit the 'like', 'tweet' and 'share' buttons, which in turn will increase your rankings. If you have already posted a couple of blogs on your website but don't know why they aren't getting noticed, it may be time for you to check the content.

Don't Forget to Link Your Inner Pages

One of the most common mistakes is being made by SEO executives is linking their home or landing page and ignoring doing the same for their inner page. Yes, your homepage is one of the most crucial pages of your website, but this doesn't mean that it is the only page you should focus on.

Because the inner pages are where the real content is, make sure to link these pages as well. If you are not fully satisfied with your website's structure, take some time to improve it and use the right keywords for its pages. This practice won't only make it easier for Google's spiders to crawl through your website, it will also make it easier for your customers and visitors to find you.

For Your Email Marketing

According to a recent report, 97% of small businesses use email marketing to connect with their respective customers. This proves that email marketing has become an essential part of targeting clients and prospects online. Now though there are several aspects that make up an effective email strategy or campaign, it is important that you focus on techniques that will increase your open rates. Here are some tips and tricks to help you pull that off. Since mobile phones and tablets have gained wider appeal the actual open rates of emails has gone up because receivers are more likely to read the emails from their mobile device than wait to arrive home or back at the office.

Time Your Emails Carefully

Even though timing isn't everything, you need to make sure that you time your emails carefully. If you don't consider the element of time when you plan your email strategy, your emails will be lost in the crowd. For example, if you send them too early in the morning, they will get lost in a bundle of other emails that were sent late at night or very early. Likewise, if you send your email too late in the afternoon, it will probably not be read because most people catch up on their emails while still at work.

So when is the right time to send the emails? According to experts, the best time to send in your company or business emails would be in the early hours of noon because the receiver will have a higher chance of reading them during a lunch break. You can also try experimenting with time frames and analyze the results so that you can rest assured that your emails aren't being wasted.

Improve Your Signup Process

When planning your email strategy, you need to focus on your signup process and ensure that it is made simple for your customers. Don't make your customers go through tiring marketing materials or steps before they sign up for your email alerts since doing so will result in nothing but a negative impression.

The best strategy that you could implement in this case is to provide a fulfillment piece or white paper as a take away and then market according to their requirements. Remember: The more refined and improved your targeted emails are, the more likely you are to achieve success with your email campaign.

Limit Your Email Receivers

Your email marketing strategy shouldn't only be about sending bulk emails to a long list of subscribers. Instead, depending upon the email service you use, you should know which emails are bouncing and which subscribers aren't opening your emails at all.

If you know which subscribers aren't reading your email, it is time for you to revise your list because they are causing the campaign to drop down. You shouldn't permanently strike off subscribers' email accounts because they are not reading your emails.

Allow Subscribers to Opt Out

If you don't want to annoy your customers to the extent that you have to protect your brand, give them the option of opting out. This is important because if your customers can't find this option easily, they will think that your company is unreliable and will end up marking you as spam.

Because your subscribers will revoke permission one way or the other, it would be better for you and your company to give a clear and straightforward option for customers to stop receiving your emails. In due time, your email open rate will increase because you will only be sending emails to the people who really do want to read them.

Keep Up With Your Competitors

Anybody who is even remotely familiar with marketing knows that it is vital to keep track of what your competitors are doing and how they are doing it. The same is true for email marketing.

If you want to save your time and resources, you must make sure that you include competitive intelligence as a part of the process. The easiest way to do this is to sign up for your competitors' emails and newsletters. This will give you a chance to keep track of what they are saying, how they are crafting their emails and other valuable information that you can use for your own email marketing strategy.

Test Your Email Marketing

What works for your competitors may not work for you. So even though you should keep track of what's going on in the industry, you should keep testing and retesting your marketing strategy. These procedures are vital for your success because the responses of your clients and customers will change over time.

Experts suggest that you keep testing everything from the time you send the email to the end of the week. This will help you analyze your campaign properly and ultimately improve or change it if needed.

For Your Social Media

With the benefits of social media marketing in mind, it is important that you learn how to target your audience. Because social media platforms are rather large, you will find that a lot of your competitors are already there and have a decent following. So you must make an effort to start your marketing properly. Go through the following tips and you'll have the opportunity to start on the right foot.

Post Popular Content

Social media platforms are all about what you post on your business profile and how you attract your customers. Therefore, you must make sure to search for content that is most popular among the audience of your competitors so that your content has a high chance of being noticed as well.

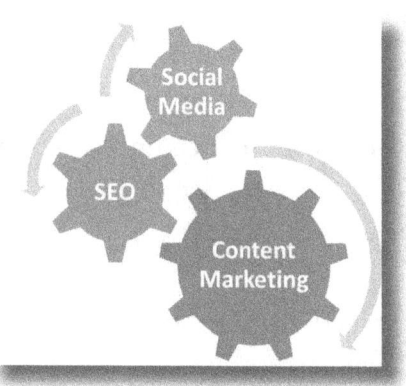

Now you shouldn't copy the content from your competitor; craft your own original content on the same topic and approach it in a different and new way. Such popular and in demand content will help show your customers that you are interested in them and that you value their views.

Limit the Number of Your Social Media Profiles

One of the most common mistakes that new businesses make when they enter social media marketing is to sign up for the services of numerous social media platforms. This is because they do not know that it is a lot better to post quality, valuable and informative content on three to four platforms rather than perform poorly on ten or fifteen different platforms.

If own more than five social media profiles, you might find it difficult to make a strong presence on every one of them simply because of the time involved. What you should do is to pinpoint the platforms that are most relevant to your business, such as Facebook, Twitter, LinkedIn and YouTube, and start posting where your audience is already hanging out. If you are finding it difficult to decide which platforms you should go for, rely on your competitors and the websites that they are on.

Always Answer Queries

Whether you are on Facebook, Twitter or any other website, you must always respond to questions and comments as quickly as possible. Check your messages and notifications no less than twice a day as this will

demonstrate your enthusiasm and interest in interacting with your customers.

When responding to questions, comments and queries always keep them to the point and avoid making any silly mistakes because your comments will be visible to everyone unless the customer has messaged you privately. In the case of negative comments, it will be your responsibility to respond in the most professional and non-aggressive manner as this will not only give a good impression about your company, it will also cool down the angry customer.

Include Images on Your Posts

Even if you are a small and fresh business that has entered the social media industry, chances are that you already have a Facebook profile. However, if you are not seeing likes, shares or comments on the posts you are sharing, this probably means that you are wasting your time because your customers aren't fully engaged.

How do you counter that? A very simple and straightforward way to boost your engagement on Facebook and other platforms is to use relevant images that help you amplify your status updates. Because our vision receptors are naturally stronger than any other, your content will have a higher chance of getting noticed when combined with an image.

Become an Expert

Where social media is concerned, you must always make sure that you go deep and not broad. As with other fields of marketing, it is a lot better to be an expert in one or two topics or channels instead of knowing a little about 10 to 20 different things. Having such an approach on social media platforms will enable you to provide in-depth and professional advice and tips to your customers, something they will appreciate more than general information about a range of topics.

Once you have decided on the topics you want to focus on, make sure to dive into each subject and give devote a lot of time to research and analysis. This will help you learn as much as you can about each area, making you an expert.

For Your Analytics

If you have a website, it is very likely that you have Google Analytics running on it. However, there is also a very high chance that you have no idea about what to do with the data and how it can help you improve your internet marketing and understand whatever is happening on your website.

Because it is always better to start small, here are some basic but very helpful tips to help you with your website analytics.

Set Your Goals

First, you need to define clear and reachable objectives that you want for your business as well as your website. Without these goals properly set out, you are doomed to fail and your entire Google analytics will go to waste. Once you decide on your goals, know what you want your customers to do when they visit your website. This action can be as simple as signing up for your newsletter, buying something if you are running an eCommerce store or a little more complex such as filling out a questionnaire. These activities are also called goals because they will give real meaning to your analytics.

Manage Your Data

Most of the new users of Google Analytics are often confused and flustered at the overwhelming amount of data and their inability to understand it because of the way it is presented. To counter this, the best thing you can do to cut your analytics down to size is to manage them via a dashboard that contains the data you need for your company. This dashboard will consist of lists that tell you where your customers or visitors are coming from, the keywords that are used the most and information about the referring website as well. Some of these websites also have a summary of your goals, which will help you to better understand analytics.

Set Up Video Event Tracking

As mentioned earlier, videos are an extremely important part of your internet marketing strategy. Therefore, if you have one or more videos on your company website, you must get a report of how many people are interacting with your video content and how they are doing it. These analytics will help you find out about events such as pressing the play, rewind, pause and stop buttons and also tell you how much time was spent interacting with the video. However, when setting this, make sure that you have your web developer on the job to properly integrate tracking code into the web pages.

Focus on Internal Searches

When a visitor comes to your website, they will often be looking for specific products or information, driving them to search for these using your internal search engine. If you set your analytics to track these searches, they will help you identify valuable information about what your visitors are specifically searching for. It will also show you what these visitors did after they searched and how long they stayed on your website.

Check if All Your Pages are Being Tracked

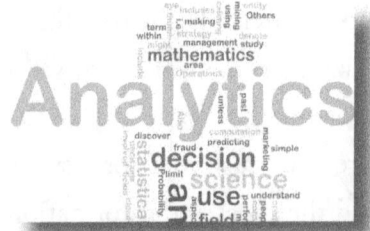

Even though this may seem a little too obvious, a lot of new Google analytics users forget to check if all their pages are being tracked. So, to be on the safe side, make sure that you have integrated the tracking code for reporting on all the pages instead of just a few. Double check all the pages by using an automatic site audit tool.

Knowing these tips, tricks and methods for improving each of your internet marketing components is essential for the growth and glory of your business. So before you start to do anything big, just implement these tips and search for more things that you can do to get the most out of your marketing plan.

Now that you know almost everything that needs to be done in internet marketing, head on to the next section to discover the things that you need to cautious about or else your efforts and planning will be futile.

Chapter Summary

After discovering the elements of internet marketing and the types of campaigns you could go for, it was time to start your marketing campaign. This chapter highlighted the ways you can start your campaign by tackling each element.

CHAPTER FIVE

Things You Should Be Cautious About in Internet Marketing

Internet marketing, if done correctly, can be an enormously beneficial and effective tool for your company and brand. Unfortunately, there are more than a handful of people who continue to make mistakes that are too common and obvious.

Avoiding these mistakes will help you plan an internet marketing strategy that is ideal and perfect. Here are some of the mistakes that you need to be aware of.

1. Not Having a Strategy

New internet marketers often end up using tools and software that are available for free but without having a real strategy or plan. By using every technology that they are presented with, these marketers are only wasting their time on tools that are not needed by their brand or company.

However, successful marketers know that to reach the internet marketing goal that they have set, they need to have a proper strategy they can follow. Tactics and tools without a plan will be useless for the growth of your business.

2. Not Knowing Your Audience

Another rookie mistake made by marketers is that of not knowing their audience. If you don't know who you are catering to, you won't know how to appeal to them.

To avoid this sort of mistake, you should always take some time and figure out who your customers are and what they like and appreciate. A number of tools such as Google's Ad Planner will help you develop a greater understanding of the data and demographics collected from your customers.

3. Not Listening Before You Speak

One of the greatest benefits of internet marketing is getting to publish your thoughts and ideas to your audience without having to pay a hefty price for it. This is why a lot of internet marketers launch their social media presence without ever listening to their audience.

A good way to remedy this is to really know your customers and solve the common problems that they are facing. Doing your homework by using one of several online listening tools will help you personalize your website and social media pages, making them an instant success.

4. Not Paying Attention to Web Analytics

Web analytics is one of the aspects you cannot ignore at any cost. Internet marketing has enabled you to measure your marketing efforts, so you know exactly what works and what doesn't. Specialized tools such as Google Analytics tell you exactly how many people came to your website and what they did to improve and enhance your marketing campaign. In short, ignoring your internet marketing's web analytics will cause you to miss out on a great deal.

5. Not Combining the Elements of Internet Marketing

Even though the six elements of internet marketing mentioned earlier come with their own strategies and best practices, thinking of them as a completely separate entity will make you miss the bigger picture. Because the efforts of search and social are highly interconnected, it is important that you combine all of these together.

New marketers should always think of online marketing as a system of many disciplines working together to achieve the same end result. However, to achieve this, you must have at least some basic understanding of the marketing channels concerned.

6. Not Making Social Connections

Another big mistake internet marketers make is not making a connection with customers and prospects that they have online. Taking the time to research and help your customers isn't the only thing that needs to be done. Unless you can make proper social connections, you won't be able to keep your current customers. So once you have a decent following on Facebook, Twitter and other social media websites, make sure that you put in the effort to really know your customers and form relationship with them.

7. Not Having Good Offers and Calls to Action

People who are new to internet marketing often don't have calls to action on their websites, which is a big disadvantage. These websites rarely have good offers that are according to the interests and likes of their prospects. Moreover, the developers of these websites don't focus on user friendliness or other such important features because they have no idea about its importance.

If you really want your internet marketing to perform well and ensure that people contact you, then you must help them solve their challenges and give them a good reason to contact you. Place great offers on your website and talk about them on your social media pages and you'll eventually begin to attract more customers than before.

8. Not Considering Load Time

Your customers expect your website and blog to load quickly. If you are on a server that is too slow or are using graphics that

take more than a minute to download, you can say goodbye to your potential customers. To market your brand effectively, focus on your load time and make sure that you put your information in front of people quickly.

9. Not Using Viral Marketing

It is extremely cost effective to have your customer market your brand for you. Word of mouth or viral marketing is known to be beneficial for a lot of companies and it is one of the best ways to make people rely on and trust your company.

Though it is important that you focus on other factors and strategies of internet marketing, not paying attention to viral marketing will make you miss out on many customers that you could have enticed.

10. Not Trying Out New Opportunities

Internet marketing is one of the fields that allow you to test and try out your new ideas. You shouldn't make the mistake of committing to one approach when you know that you can constantly try out new ideas and see how they perform in the real world. Remember that unless you try these ideas and techniques, you won't be able to see their actual results and benefits.

Being cautious and careful about these common internet marketing mistakes will help you in making a name for your brand and company. However, these tips aren't the only ones that you should consider because you'll learn a lot more as you move ahead in your business.

Chapter Summary

With the right kind of techniques, internet marketing can be an amazing and effective feature of your business. However, there are some common mistakes that you must look out for, especially those tackled in this Book.

- *Not having an internet marketing strategy*
- *Not knowing more about your audience*
- *Not listening before you speak*
- *Not paying attention to web analytics*
- *Not combining the elements of internet marketing*
- *Not making strong social connections*
- *Not offering good promotions and call to actions*
- *Not considering loading time*
- *Not using viral marketing*
- *Not trying out new opportunities*

CHAPTER SIX

Myths and Facts Surrounding Internet Marketing

There are a lot of myths surrounding internet marketing. Since a lot of these are made popular by experts, it is difficult to separate  reality from lies and know exactly how to proceed. To help you make the most of your internet marketing strategies, here are the truths behind some well-known myths.

MYTH #1: MY TARGET MARKET IS OLDER SO I DON'T NEED SOCIAL MEDIA

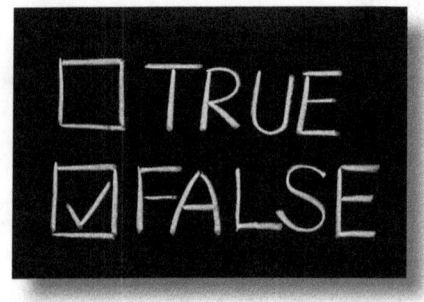 **Fact:** The idea that you don't need social media marketing because your target audience is old is one of the most common myths. Several studies have shown that more than 52% of online boomers and 32% of online adults are using popular social networking websites. Facebook and Twitter are at the top of list while LinkedIn follows closely. So don't miss out on the opportunity to connect and build a relationship with senior members who have been waiting for your business to come to social media.

MYTH #2: EMAIL MARKETING DOESN'T WORK ANYMORE

Fact: Even though VoIP has replaced email for personal communication, businesses are still benefiting from this technology. Building your own mail list and providing a focused and properly executed email marketing campaign is very effective and will help you with your internet marketing. Once you learn how to create and deliver quality content to your customer's inbox, you'll start to welcome new visitors and members.

MYTH #3: ANYONE CAN BUILD MY WEBSITE

Fact: Because your website is the foundation of your inbound marketing activities, you need to make sure that you design and develop something professional that your customers will appreciate. Even though it is true that you can create a professional website just by using a premium theme, choosing the color palette, adding your company logo and writing content are crucial to reach out to your customers. So invest in your company website and start transforming your potentials into customers right away.

MYTH #4: GREAT INTERNET MARKETING GETS INSTANT RESULTS

Fact: Though marketing creates visibility and a few tactics produce instant results, marketing is all about maintaining contact with your target audience and ensuring that they know who you are and what you do. It

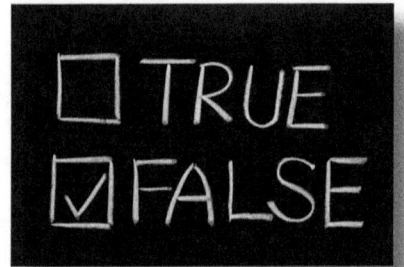

may be days, weeks, or even months before you get the results that you are looking for. However, rest assured that once you start seeing results, they'll be a lot more than you expected.

Myth #5: Facebook Is All You Need

Fact: Sure, Facebook is the largest social networking website today, but you do need to market your brand on other websites as well. The reason for this is simple: What if your Facebook marketing doesn't work? What if most of your customers don't like using this platform? Therefore, even if you are on Facebook, make sure that you are integrating other platforms as well. What if you Facebook site is blocked for some reason? That means your one and only marketing medium is unavailable.

Myth #6: Internet Marketing Is Only For Big Companies

Fact: This cannot be further from the truth. Because internet marketing has become such an essential part of businesses, it is a necessity for companies big and small. Even though the techniques and methods used for them will vary slightly, small businesses will need to implement internet marketing as well.

Myth #7: You Don't Need Money for Internet Marketing

Fact: When you advertise your brand or company on media channels such as the radio and TV, you wouldn't expect the service to be free, would you? So don't listen to people who say that internet marketing is free. The service is cheap and convenient, but it won't be free.

Myth #8: You Need To Be On the First Page of Google

Fact: Though Google is the best and most popular search engine on the internet, you don't necessarily need to be on the first page to get noticed. Because Google only has a couple of spots available on the first page, it will be unrealistic and impossible for you to always reach the first page. So instead of reaching for the impossible, try to just get yourself at least indexed and you'll soon be able to reach the first few pages of search engine results.

Internet marketing is all about creating visibility for your brand and business by educating your prospects and customers about your products and services and the various ways in which you can help them solve a problem. Therefore, everything you do to accomplish this for your company is a successful internet marketing strategy that deserves all the time, effort, energy and resources that you have.

The only way you can know the difference between myth and fact is if you spend time researching and experimenting with internet marketing. So never limit your education to this book since the world of internet marketing is always changing and evolving.

Chapter Summary

Internet marketing is not devoid of myths that are made up by people who don't know how to use it properly. The chapter on the myths of internet marketing uncovered the following truths.

- *You shouldn't ignore social media marketing just because your target audience is older.*

- *Email marketing is still one of the best ways to get your messages through to your customers.*

- *Your business website is the first place your customer or prospect will visit.*

- *No matter what kind of internet marketing you go for, it will take you sometime to properly begin to see the results.*

- *When focusing on social media marketing, don't just pay attention to Facebook because there are plenty of other websites that you can try out as well.*

- *Internet marketing works for big as well as small businesses.*

- *Even though a lot of features of internet marketing will be free, it is not something that won't require any budget at all.*

- *Don't be obsessed with getting your name on the first page of Google's search engine results. There is only so much space on the first few pages of Google and that is mostly given to multinational companies that have been in the industry for a long time.*

CHAPTER SEVEN

How to Keep Track of Your Internet Marketing

Internet marketing is more than just getting your word out there. Apart from attracting customers with witty marketing antics and creative plans, you also need to be able to track your results. In fact, there is no point in creating an incredible marketing strategy if you don't even know which parts of it have worked.

So how do you track the success of a marketing strategy? Now you may think that the answer to this is to use analytical tools; though this may be true, there are a whole lot of other things that you can do as well. The following tips will introduce you to effective methods that can help you track your internet marketing.

Tip #1: Ask Your Customers

When tracking the efficiency of your online or offline marketing efforts, one of the most effective but overlooked methods is asking your customers directly. Create and ask short yet meaningful questions such as "Where did you hear about us?" and you will gain a lot of information. Asking these questions will help you discover which of your marketing methods is getting you the most traffic and which you should drop already.

Tip #2: Subscribe to Google Alerts

One of the common analytical tools used by companies to track their online marketing is Google Alerts. This is a simple yet very powerful service that emails you every time a new result comes up on your keyword, topic or query. For example, if you provide car hire services in a local area and they type in the suburb name followed by 'car hire' in the Google search box, this tool will email you. Subscribing to this service is easy because you can do it via RSS, which enables you to track everything ranging from news to videos.

Tip #3: Consider Using Trackable Phone Numbers and Others

Phone tracking is easy and highly efficient when it comes to measuring the efficiency your online marketing strategies. All you need to do is to place your number on your website, email or social media page and then track the exact number of calls being made through each marketing tool. Using  this technique will help you gain great insight into your marketing strategy and help you identify the areas generating the most traffic.

You can also use links for certain online campaigns. These links are especially effective with social media because you can place them easily on Facebook and Twitter and assess how many clicks they generate.

Tip #4: Use Blog Search

Another great way to find out the results of your internet marketing efforts is to subscribe to blog search engines. Simply type in your company's name or brand and you'll find out exactly who is blogging about  you. One of the greatest benefits of this analytical tool is that it tells you the good as well as the bad. This means that once you put in your URL and keywords into the Google Blog search bar, you'll know exactly who is saying what about you.

Tip #5: Try Out Social Mention

If most of your internet marketing is focused on social media, you should consider trying out SocialMention. This tool is one of the best available these days because it'll search whoever mentioned you through blog comments, video, bookmarks, news, events, and much more. Relatively similar to Google Alerts, this service allows you to subscribe to this service via RSS or email.

Tip #7: Track Landing Pages

 If you are running online promotions and would like to know about results, tracking the landing pages of your website is just what you need to do. You can also make this work by generating a custom landing page which has a short and easy URL that

people can remember. Once this custom landing page is live, you can use Google Analytics to watch how much traffic goes into the website and how successful your internet marketing campaign is.

However, while creating these customer landing pages, make sure not to put the same content from your main website on the domains. Even though it may be a very tempting thought, this will only cause you trouble because you'll run the risk of being penalized by Google for duplicate content. So if you really want to see results with while using custom landing pages, make sure that each of them is as unique as possible.

Tip #8: Keep Tabs with Tools like Hootsuite and Sendible

There are many online tools designed to help you managed and monitor your social media marketing. Products like Hootsuite, Sendible and Tracksur offer various features such as monitoring, posting and alerts.

Tip #9: Use Specialized Tools like SEO Monitor

It's important to place monitoring on your websites. There are many products in the marketplace including SEO Monitor, SEOMoz and SEMrush.

Tips #10: Benefit From Sentiment Metrics

You can also benefit from Sentiment Metrics. This service offers companies a comprehensive reputation management tool that digs into the information from forums, photo sharing and video websites, and social networks to tell you what people are saying about you and your brand.

One of the most interesting things about Sentiment Metrics is that it also indicates the emotion in the information that it finds, hence the name 'Sentiment'. The data that is being provided will either be positive, neutral or negative. Moreover, with Sentiment Metrics, you will be provided with a few easy-to-read graphics and charts which will help you in keeping track of all the news that they find about you.

Tracking your company's online campaigns can be tough, but it is possible with the right strategies, tools and methods. With the help of the tips and tools in this chapter, you will know exactly how many of your internet marketing efforts have paid off.

Chapter Summary

Here are a couple of things that will help you in keeping track of your internet marketing along with your analytical tools.

- *Asking your customers*
- *Subscribing to Google Alerts*
- *Using trackable phone numbers*
- *Using blog searches*
- *Trying out Social Mention*
- *Tracking landing pages effectively*
- *Keep tabs with BoardTracker*
- *Try tools like Filtrbox*
- *Explore Sentiment Metrics*

CHAPTER EIGHT

The Latest Trends of Internet Marketing

Internet marketing in 2013 and 2014 can be summed up in a few words: Google updates, mobile and big brands. As you look back at the events that shaped that year when it comes to online marketing, it is also important to look forward and wonder what trends will show up in 2015 and beyond.

Because there are different aspects of online marketing, it's hard to know what is important and what should be left alone. However, there are a few critical areas where you should invest your time and money. The following sections highlight those.

CONTENT MATTERS TO GOOGLE

If your business has been around for two or more years, you are probably aware of a major change in SEO. Unfortunately, for some companies this change has meant a drop in organic search website traffic while for others it is a breath of fresh air.

In the last couple of years, Google has released three major updates: Panda, Penguin and Hummingbird. Though there have been a lot of changes implemented with these, one thing has remained constant: Google's appreciation of quality content. The search engine thinks highly of content that people find interesting, giving websites hosting it high ranks. So what does this mean for you? It means that you should start creating blog posts, videos, slide shows and other types of content that will help in educating, informing or enlightening your audience. Once published, simply watch your ranking go up.

Focus on Mobile Devices

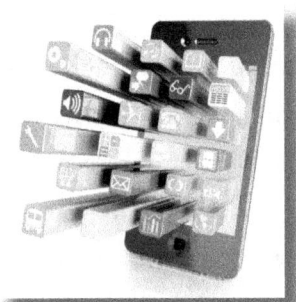

A recent study has estimated that by the year 2017, 68% of the US population will be using a smartphone. These numbers are likely to be the same in Australia as well. Because mobile devices are changing the way people access information, you must make sure that you are available on them. If your company provides the information that your customers are looking for, you'll get the opportunity to grow.

Going mobile will help your company access your customers anywhere and anytime - when they are commuting to work or while they are out shopping for some essentials. Optimising your marketing strategy for that new reality will prepare you for marketing success.

Design is Crucial

If you think that developing your business website is the only thing you need to do to attract online traffic, you have been misled. At

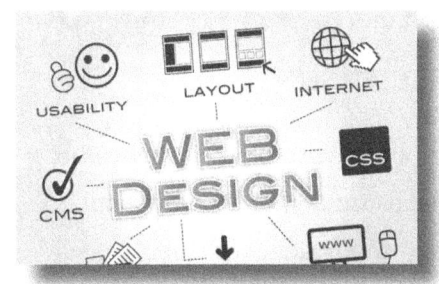

present, there is a higher importance placed on design and user friendliness. Because customers want information real fast (within five seconds), websites of big and small companies need to keep pace with client demands or else they will lose the people that they are trying to target. So don't think that design and usability are unnecessary elements for your internet marketing strategy because they are quickly becoming an essential part of marketing efforts.

Video, Video, Video

Statistics have shown that more than one billion different users visit YouTube each month. This number is increasing at an alarmingly high rate. Internet users from all over the world are watching thousands of videos and are demanding even more. Search engine giants such as Google are also starting to feature top video search results on regular search results and via a separate link.

Creating and developing product videos, testimonials and demonstrations online can all be a part of your successful internet marketing strategy. Don't wait for your competitors find out about the advantages of these videos and start earning new customers right now.

Rely on Social Media Audiences

Though every business relies on its customers, only a few realize the importance of their social media audience. Social media don't only present businesses with a good opportunity to generate an audience with no location barriers; they also give them the chance to learn from them.

Build an audience of followers on Facebook and Twitter and check up on how these people are interacting with your company's fan page. Social media can be a great way for businesses to know more about their customers so that they can serve them better.

Keep Up With Google

In the past, Google said that its professionals tweak its algorithm almost twice a day. Though these changes aren't easy to notice, those mentioned officially do have an impact on the internet marketing community.

Studies that were conducted last year show that there were at least 15 important changes made to Google in 2013 and 2014. Therefore, it is clear that to remain in the top search results of Google, you must keep yourself up-to-date on the various changes that are taking place.

Try Out HTML 5

In the last year, HTML 5 has done more than just take over Flash and other plug-ins, it has made trends of its own. If you have never experimented with HTML5, you should know that it is compatible with multiple browsers, devices, and screens and doesn't require external plug-ins such as Flash to play interactive content.

So don't just sit there and expect your users to install Flash because your website requires it. Instead, give them an HTML 5 website that is compatible with everything and everywhere.

Show Your Interest with Pinterest

If your target audience consists of females aged between 18 and 64, Pinterest is surely the place to be. They have over 70 million users and growing with an average of over 5 million daily pins.

One of the most amazing things about Pinterest users is that its users are actually active, unlike the case with Twitter and Facebook. More than 21 million of 70 million people accessed and used their account at least once in a month, which means that you do have the chance of growth. So don't wait on the sidelines while your competitors take your place; take a step forward right away.

Less is More

One of the most notable changes that you'll notice is the shift in consumer preferences regarding simple marketing messages instead of ones that are difficult to understand and comprehend. If you think about Google, Apple and the messages of other such big corporations, you'll notice that they now value simplicity and it is one of the top reasons why they are appreciated.

What small businesses can learn from this is not to waste their time in creating information, and advertisements that beg to attract attention but to design innovative and creative messages that don't overwhelm the reader.

Age of Ad Retargeting

Ad retargeting is the process which is used by businesses to track the websites that the users have visited. Once a user leaves a particular website, the product or service they viewed or gained information about will be shown to them again through the advertisements of different web pages.

It is obvious why and how the technique can be so effective in the world of internet marketing. Even though only 2% of web traffic is converted on the first visit, ad retargeting gives you the chance to increase the overall conversion rate by reminding your customers of the products that they have just viewed. Because this keeps you and your brand in their mind, you'll have a much higher chance of converting the visitors.

Interconnectivity of Social Signals and SEO

Even though social signals still don't carry the same weight as traditional SEO, it is true that they play a very important role in search engine rankings. This is mainly because Google and other search engines believe in providing the users with the most relevant and high quality content. So basically, the more people share your piece of content, the higher your likelihood of getting noticed by Google and making it to their top positions.

Moreover, integrating these social share buttons will also be beneficial for your brand's reliability because these shares will serve as a stamp of approval for visitors that have come to the page. If these visitors see that the content they are viewing already has hundreds or even thousands

of shares, they'll be more likely to appreciate your brand.

Email Marketing Has Reemerged

A lot of new minds in the internet marketing business think that email marketing is dead because of social media. However, this is very far away from the truth. In fact, if you were to analyze the email marketing situation of today, you would find that the customer click rate has increased in recent years.

For example, if you have a product to sell and sent an email to prospects 10 years ago, it would have had a much lesser chance of being interacted with than one that is sent today. Because the internet has gotten somewhat safer, people are more likely to try out the deal, promotion, or product that you are offering.

Loyalty Marketing in Focus

In the last couple of years, you must have heard big brands announce that their key focus is on their loyal customers. Everywhere you look more and more loyalty teams are popping up and marketers are having a hard time understanding customer loyalty and what to do with them. If you don't want to be one of these people then you must understand the meaning of reciprocal loyalty.

Basically, in this type of marketing, not only are your customers loyal to your brand, you have the responsibility of returning back the favor by presenting the customers them with a personalized experience and excellent customer service.

There are many cloud based loyalty solutions on the market which can automate the process of maintaining a strategy.

Innovative Changes

Gone are the times when people used to do one thing in the same boring way. Both businesses and customers are looking for innovation and creativity in their work. This is why some of the biggest companies today are focusing on growing teams that are dedicated to innovation, creative thinking, and challenging the age old protocols that were made in a very different age from today.

Even if you have a small to medium sized company, you can always just hire a couple of talented, skilled, and creative people and give them the resources that they need to build something better.

Increased Use of Gamification

Creating and applying game design thinking to applications in order to make them more fun and engaging has been growing at a fast rate. Big brands, which have nothing to do with games, are spending more money and resources on making their products and services fun and attention grabbing.

If you too would like to make your application or website match games, there are plenty of tools and platforms that you could try which will help you out.

Keeping up with the trends and following at least a few of them will make your internet marketing more likely to succeed. Because all the areas of internet marketing are always changing in one way or the other, it is important that you keep checking and researching about it. But don't worry about the difficulty or challenges of the alterations because they are designed not only to be beneficial for your customers, but for your business as well.

Chapter Summary

In chapter 8, we talked about the evergreen and new trends of internet marketing.

1. Always work and update your website and blog content according to the requirements of Google and other search engines. The quality of your content will determine whether or not your website appears in organic searches, so make sure that you don't leave it behind.

2. Optimizing your website for mobile devices is a necessity in a time when people are all about smartphones.

3. It is crucial that you pay attention to the design of your website because your visitors will turn away immediately if they don't see a professionally designed page.

4. Create testimonials, demonstrations and product videos then post them on YouTube and other video website. Videos are now quickly becoming viral and if you aren't using them yet then chances are high that your competitors are using it to beat you.

5. Social media marketing is more than just getting your word out there. With your profiles and fan pages on websites like Facebook, Twitter, and LinkedIn, you get the chance to learn from how the customers are interacting with the posts and content that you have given them.

6. If you want to remain in the results of Google, you must keep up with its updates. Though there are almost two consistent tweaks that are daily that are done to the algorithm, there are

only a few changes that are noticeable and should be taken into account.

7. Skip old school Flash player and think about designing your website using the HTML5.

8. Make yourself heard and known by your audience by being on Pinterest. This is a social platform that is slowly but surely making its way to the top.

9. Simplistic design and content are all the rage right now. Don't make the mistake of thinking that your audience will appreciate a complex marketing message that they need to think about because people don't have the time to comprehend the meaning anymore.

10. Companies all over the world have started to use ad retargeting as an effort to remain in the minds of their visitors and customers.

11. You must know that social signals and SEO are more interconnected now than they ever were. Because Google believes in providing visitors and customers the best service and information, they will show preference for websites and blogs that have been shared or liked multiple times.

12. It maybe the age of mobile, but this doesn't mean that email marketing is completely dead. In fact, analyzing the data of email marketing today and that of a few years ago has shown that the click rate has increased considerably.

13. Loyalty marketing is what is required from all businesses. Learn to use these loyal customers for your benefit.

14. The age old internet marketing techniques will no longer work with your customers. This is why you need to be as innovative and creative with your strategies as you can.

15. Gamification in designing apps and programs is another necessity and trend that you cannot do without.

up with its updates. Though there are almost always two consistent tweaks that are made daily to the algorithm, there are only a few changes that are noticeable and should be taken into account.

16. Skip old school Flash player and think about designing your website using the HTML5.

17. Make yourself heard and known by your audience by being on Pinterest. This is a social platform that is slowly but surely making its way to the top.

18. Simplistic design and content are all the rage right now. Don't make the mistake of thinking that your audience will appreciate a complex marketing message that they need to think about because people don't have the time to comprehend the meaning anymore.

19. Companies all over the world have started to use ad retargeting in an effort to remain in the minds of their visitors and customers.

20. You must know that social signals and SEO are more interconnected now than they ever were. Because Google believes in

providing visitors and customers the best service and information, they will show preference for websites and blogs that have been shared or liked multiple times.

21. *It maybe the age of mobile, but this doesn't mean that email marketing is completely dead. In fact, analyzing the data of email marketing today and that of a few years ago has shown that the click rate has increased considerably.*

22. *Loyalty marketing is what is required from all businesses. Learn to use these loyal customers for your benefit.*

23. *The age old internet marketing techniques will no longer work with your customers. This is why you need to be as innovative and creative with your strategies as you can.*

24. *Gamification in designing apps and programs is another necessity and trend that you cannot do without.*

CHAPTER NINE

Enhancing Your Current Internet Marketing

Internet marketing is a process that constantly needs to be upgraded or else it will fail to attract the attention that you are looking for. Therefore, even if you apply basic internet marketing strategies, it is crucial that you continue to enhance and improve them to stay ahead of the competition. To ensure that you make the right decisions, here are a few tips and tricks that you can add.

Post Daily Content on Social Media

One of the easiest ways to enhance your social and internet marketing is to post content consistently. Several studies have shown that because audiences react to different positing frequencies, you must test the optimal frequency first. The ideal number of posts for Facebook shouldn't be less than one to two and you must make sure that you post content on Twitter at least four to six times a day.

The time at which you post the content on Facebook or other social media pages is also important. If you post too late at night, your customers may not have the opportunity to view it when they wake up the next day. So when making a social media strategy for your internet marketing, always consider the time frame.

Run a Campaign

Running campaigns on your company website or social media pages is one of the best ways to attract potential customers. If you like the idea of developing a campaign, make sure that you pay attention to the initial message as well as the prize being offered since your customers or visitors won't be interested unless they can win something worth their time and effort.

Because every campaign must have some terms and conditions, you should clearly state them. Among other important aspects, your campaign must highlight the start and end date of the competition, the prize details, and the objective or goal that is meant to be achieved.

Consider Running a Twitter Q&A

A technique that you can try to grow your Twitter followers and increase their engagement dramatically is running a weekly Q&A session. Pick any day of the week and encourage your Twitter users to post questions related to your products and services. This method won't only give you a chance to resolve your customers' queries, it may also give you a chance to blog about the questions that you feel are most common.

With time, as more people begin to interact with these sessions, you will get the opportunity to establish your brand as an authority in the business. You can also use hashtags related to the Q&A and ask your customers to use them in their tweets as well.

Experiment with Blog Titles

You already know that the title of your content carries a lot of weight. Unfortunately, a lot of businesses don't yet realize that the title of their blog post carries a lot more weight than they think, which is why they don't give it as much attention as the content of the post. While it is important that you research and write a professionally sound blog post, you must use unique, catchy and everyday language while creating the content of headline.

Let Infographics Take Charge

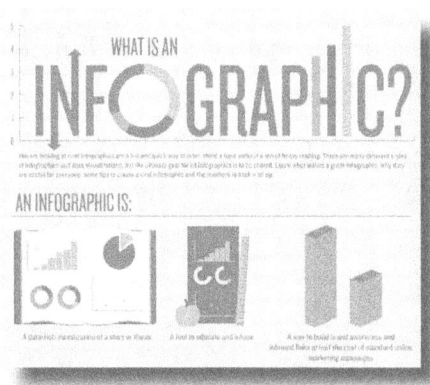

Infographics have become very popular over the last few years and should be implemented in your internet marketing strategy. This is because infographics are widely appreciated for numerous reasons such as the ease of absorbing the information highlighted in the image. So if you want to start attracting a lot of traffic to your website or need to get a number of high value backlinks, make sure that you invest in a professionally designed infographic. Also, ensure that it's well-researched and relevant to your industry and customers; dig deep to find out the areas that your customers are really interested in and find a whole lot of points and statistics that can be covered.

You can easily create Infographics using cloud solutions such as visual.ly or piktochart.com.

Improve Customer Services

Your customer services must be impeccable. This isn't only applicable to your company website, but also on your social media platforms. If a visitor replies to your tweet or messages you on Facebook, they expect you to give them a prompt reply. So if you fail to respond to them, you will end up losing their trust.

Because of your lack of communication and attention, an unhappy customer will turn towards your competitors and ask them for help.

However, if you improve and work on your customer services, you will be able to deliver a prompt and thoughtful reply in a timely manner. This will flatter and interest your customer, who will begin trusting your brand even more. So make sure that you assign someone to this particular task and ask them to be as creative as they can with their answers.

Embrace Mistakes and Errors

Your customers know that mistakes are unavoidable. The truth of this fact increases tenfold when it comes to the world of social media. However, instead of ignoring or not admitting these mistakes, embrace them in the most modest of ways. Though you don't need to re-tweet or re-post if you miss a comma or two, it is necessary to correct larger mistakes. Errors such as overcharging customer credit cards and misleading product descriptions should be proactively responded to with an apology along with an explanation.

However, what if you make a really big and embarrassing mistake? In such a case, it will be best not to crawl into a hole of embarrassment. Instead, come up with a really creative, funny and intriguing thing to say and cover the situation a little.

Change the Formatting and Appearance of Your Content

You should realize that only a fraction of those who visit your website or blog will have the time and patience to go through an entire post. Instead of reading every word of it, they may prefer to merely scan the content for the information that they need. These visitors, who are also known as 'scanners', will often scroll down the page and only read the words or phrases that really jump out and catch their attention.

This is why it is important that you post and create content that makes use of several formatting features such as bold, italic and highlighting. However, make sure that you don't overwhelm your content by using a lot of these; everyone will think that you are trying too hard, which will have the exact opposite effect of what you are trying to achieve. You should also try to divide the content using subheadings and bullet lists so that it is easier for readers to pinpoint the areas they are interested in reading.

Send Out an Email Newsletter

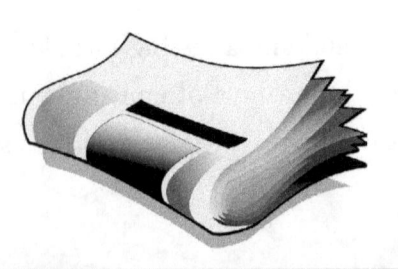

As you know by now, email marketing is a very important part of your internet marketing. One of the things that are most crucial in email marketing is a newsletter as it gives out valuable information to your customers. Sending out email newsletters is a powerful and effective way to stay in touch with your customers on a regular basis, so it must be a part of your internet marketing. When you send your customers these newsletters, you will stay on their radar and the next time they need a particular product or service, they will turn to your brand.

A quality email newsletter is one of the best customer retention tools. It can also be a very cost effective customer acquisition program if used in the correct way. If you're wondering what the right way is, it is including helpful tips and tricks, special offers, campaigns, news about recent products, and free stuff that you'll be offering customers in the future.

Hire a Public Relations Agency

If you want to improve and enhance your internet marketing campaign, you should also think about hiring a good public relations agency as it will help you boost the visibility and profitability of your business. One of the key roles of a PR agency is creating news, press releases and articles and sending them to different media where they can be published.

Hiring a PR agency that knows its way around the right media can prove to be quite advantageous because it will help you get your word out to the customers. When searching for such an agency, make sure that you look for one that is experienced enough to know the ins and outs of your industry.

Create Business Cards with your Website URL

You can also enhance your internet marketing strategies by combining them with some traditional marketing efforts. For example, displaying your company website URL on the back or front of your business card and leaving it in different places such as restaurants and sports centres will increase the likelihood of people finding the things you are offering. Though most of your customers are online, you can also find a lot of them offline as well.

ADD AN FAQ SECTION TO YOUR WEBSITE

If you don't have an FAQ section on your website yet, you should create one as soon as possible. Implementing a frequently asked questions section will be even more crucial if your customers tend to ask the same questions repeatedly. This simple and straightforward addition will let your readers know that you are not just listening to them, but also responding effectively and long before they contact you. Also consider creating some SAQ's or Should Ask Questions.

Because internet marketing is growing at such a high rate, it is vital that you keep improving and enhancing what you already have and add the things you think are likely to help your marketing.

Chapter Summary

After creating your internet marketing campaign, you need to enhance it regularly to ensure that no stone is left unturned. In this chapter, we highlighted some excellent methods to help you do that.

- *Post content on social media consistently.*

- *Start running a campaign on your website or social media page to attract more customers and keep the existing ones interested.*

- *Pick out a day in the week when you want your Twitter followers to ask you questions and answer them accordingly.*

- *Try out new and fresh blog titles to attract the attention of readers.*

- *Infographics are your new best friend. Choose topics which have plenty of information and statistics available and have them professionally designed.*

- *Whatever services you provide, you must always make sure that your customer services are perfect. Don't ignore your customers or resist answering their queries because this will only decrease the value of your business.*

- *Don't run or hide from any errors or mistakes that you have made on social media sites. Confront them and let your customers know that you are working to improve the situation in the best manner possible.*

- *Make your content easy to read by using different formatting tools such as italic and bold.*

- *Developing your own email newsletter and sending it out to your customers is an effective way to stay in touch with them and remain in their minds.*

- *Hiring a PR agency will help you increase your reliability in front of the media and your audience.*

- *Think about adding your company URL to your business card to improve your chances of being discovered by new customers.*

- *No website is complete without an FAQ section.*

Conclusion

Internet marketing is not something that can be ignored in this digital age. So if you really want to make your business a successful one you need to make sure to consider everything detailed in this Book. In addition, you need to be open to any new techniques to ensure that you're up-to-date and on par with, if not ahead of, your competitors.

I Wish you all the best in your future marketing endeavors and feel free to contact me at www.johnnorth.com.au or www.evolveyourbusiness.com.au for any assistance or feedback.

Also…. Don't forget our special reader offer!

REGISTER THIS BOOK NOW and I'll immediately gift you my action packed, comprehensive and life changing four part video course…**absolutely FREE**…no strings attached!

In it, amongst a literal slew of other fact-packed ideas, you'll learn the inside secrets of how to generate as many leads as your business can handle… WITHOUT spending a cent on marketing or advertising.

Visit http://bookoffer.evolveyourbusiness.com.au or

Scan this QR Code:

Resources & References

1- http://blog.getsatisfaction.com/2013/06/18/mobile_search_optimized_for_customer_experienc/

2- http://www.asymco.com/2013/12/13/how-many-americans-will-be-using-an-iphone/

3- http://index.fireclick.com/

4- http://www.pewinternet.org/2013/02/14/the-demographics-of-social-media-users-2012/

5- http://www.public.site1.mirror2.phi.emarketer.com/Articles.aspx

www.ingramcontent.com/pod-product-compliance
Lightning Source LLC
Chambersburg PA
CBHW071721170526
45165CB00005B/2099